Trading Without Sense

Adrianne Morel

Adrianne Morel

Index

Adrianne Morel

The Chaos of Trading

Trading chaos is something that many traders, especially beginners, face when venturing into the financial markets. It's easy to get carried away with the excitement of the potential for quick profits and forget the reality that trading is a complex field, full of risks and pitfalls. Imagine someone walking into a room full of screens showing constantly moving graphs, figures that change from one second to the next, and news that seems contradictory. That person, without solid knowledge or a clear plan, feels overwhelmed, caught in a whirlwind of information without knowing what to do.

Many novice traders jump into trading without adequate preparation, guided by the belief that they can dominate the markets simply with instinct or luck. However, this lack of preparation is what creates chaos. It's like trying to navigate a stormy sea without a map or a compass. Without a clear trading plan, without a defined strategy, traders find themselves reacting impulsively to market movements, instead of acting in a calculated manner. This leads to a series of hasty decisions, based more on emotions such as fear and greed, than on logical and well-informed analysis.

Chaos also arises when traders are exposed to too much information without knowing how to filter or interpret it. In the digital age, it is easy to access an overwhelming amount of data, from breaking news to complex technical analysis. But having access to so much information can be counterproductive if you don't know what is relevant and what is not. This constant bombardment of data can lead to analysis paralysis, where the trader feels unable to make decisions for fear of making a mistake, or, on the contrary, making hasty decisions based on incomplete or misinterpreted information.

Another factor that contributes to chaos is a lack of discipline. Many traders, after experiencing one or two losses, begin to doubt their strategy and begin to constantly change tactics, looking for a magic solution that will guarantee profits. This constant search for the perfect strategy, which does not exist, only fuels more disorder and confusion. Instead of sticking to a well-thought-out strategy, traders get sidetracked, losing sight of their long-term goals and falling into a cycle of losses and frustration.

Improper risk management is another source of trading chaos. Many traders, blinded by the possibility of profits, forget to set clear limits on their losses. They trade with too much leverage or risk more than they can afford to lose. When things don't go as expected, panic sets in and they make desperate decisions, which only aggravates their problems. Trading without proper risk management is like walking a tightrope without a safety net underneath; Eventually, the fall is inevitable.

Chaos also manifests itself in the lack of a proper time frame. Some traders constantly switch between different time frames in search of signals that confirm their decisions, without realizing that this practice only creates confusion and contradictions. A five-minute chart can show a completely different trend than a daily chart, and trying to match both views only leads to erratic and contradictory decisions. Without a clear understanding of the time frame in which they are trading, traders find themselves trapped in a tangle of mixed signals.

Finally, trading chaos is a direct consequence of a lack of patience. Many traders want quick results and are not willing to wait for the market to move in their favor. This impatience leads to closing trades prematurely or entering the market at inappropriate times, resulting in unnecessary losses. Patience is an essential virtue in trading, but in a chaotic environment, it is easy to lose it and fall into the trap of immediacy.

In short, trading chaos is nothing more than the result of a combination of factors such as lack of preparation, information overload, lack of discipline, inadequate risk management, confusion in time frames and impatience. For many, trading may seem like a constant battle against these elements, but understanding the roots of chaos is the first step to overcoming it. By recognizing these problems and working to correct them, it is possible to transform chaos into a more orderly and controlled process, where decisions are made with confidence and clarity, rather than fear and confusion.

Lack of a Trading Plan

The lack of a trading plan is one of the most common and harmful mistakes that traders make, especially those who are starting out in this world. It is easy to get carried away by the excitement of entering the markets and think that you can trade successfully without a defined strategy. However, this mentality often leads to failure, since operating without a plan is like sailing aimlessly, without knowing where you are going or how to get there.

A trading plan is, in essence, a set of rules and guidelines that a trader follows to make decisions in the market. It includes aspects such as the criteria for entering and exiting a trade, risk management, the amount of capital to invest, and profit and loss objectives. Having a clear and well-structured plan is crucial because it provides a framework that helps maintain discipline and avoid impulsive decisions. Without a plan, traders find themselves reacting to market movements in a haphazard manner, basing their decisions on emotions such as fear, greed or hope, rather than on rational and objective analysis.

One of the main problems with operating without a plan is the lack of consistency. Traders who do not have a plan often change their strategy constantly, looking for the magic formula that guarantees profits. This behavior not only creates confusion, but also prevents the trader from being able to properly evaluate what is working and what is not. Without a plan, each operation becomes an isolated experiment, without a solid foundation that allows us to learn from mistakes and improve over time.

Another crucial aspect of the trading plan is risk management. Many traders underestimate the importance of setting clear limits on their losses, which can lead to catastrophic situations. Without a plan outlining how much you are willing to lose on a trade, it is easy to get carried away with the hope that the market will turn in your favor, holding losing positions for longer than necessary and racking up increasing losses. A well-designed trading plan includes not only entry and exit strategies, but also strict rules on how much capital is risked on each trade, which helps protect the trader's portfolio from devastating losses.

The lack of a trading plan also negatively affects the psychology of the trader. When you don't have a plan, every trading decision is fraught with uncertainty, which creates stress and anxiety. Traders constantly worry about whether they made the right decision, whether they should have entered or exited earlier, or whether they should have used a different strategy. These types of thoughts are not only exhausting, but also lead to additional errors as the trader is trading under pressure and with an unstable mindset. A clear and well-defined trading plan helps reduce this emotional burden by providing a roadmap that the trader can follow with confidence.

Furthermore, without a trading plan, it is almost impossible to measure performance effectively. Traders need a benchmark to evaluate whether their strategies are working or not. Without a plan, there is no clear standard against which to compare results, making it difficult to identify areas for improvement or adjust strategies when necessary. A trading plan provides these benchmarks, allowing traders to keep track of their trades, analyze their decisions, and make necessary adjustments to improve their performance over time.

It is also important to note that a trading plan is not something static. Markets are constantly changing, and what works today may not work tomorrow. Therefore, a good trading plan includes the flexibility necessary to adapt to new market conditions without losing sight of the main objectives. This means that traders should review and adjust their plan regularly, based on their experience and changes in the markets, to ensure that it remains effective and relevant.

Finally, the lack of a trading plan can lead to a loss of confidence. Without a plan, every trade feels like a gamble, and losses can seriously affect a trader's morale. Over time, this lack of confidence can cause traders to doubt themselves and their ability to make profitable decisions, which in turn can lead them to abandon trading altogether. A trading plan, on the other hand, provides a solid foundation on which to build confidence. When traders trade according to a plan, they know they are making decisions based on careful analysis and well-thought-out rules, giving them the confidence to persevere even when things don't go as expected.

In short, the lack of a trading plan is one of the biggest obstacles to success in the financial markets. Without a plan, traders face inconsistency, poor risk management, psychological stress, the inability to evaluate their performance, and loss of confidence. A well-designed trading plan is essential to successfully navigate the markets, providing a clear and structured framework that allows traders to trade with discipline, confidence and clarity. By developing and following a trading plan, traders can transform chaos and uncertainty into an effective and controlled strategy, increasing their chances of long-term success.

Adrianne Morel

Uncontrolled Emotions

Uncontrolled emotions are one of the biggest enemies that any trader can face on their path to success. In the world of trading, where quick and accurate decisions are essential, getting carried away by emotions such as fear, greed, euphoria or panic can be devastating. Although it is natural to feel intense emotions when it comes to money, especially when the stakes are high, allowing these emotions to dominate your trading decisions is a recipe for disaster.

Fear is one of the most powerful emotions that affects traders. This fear can manifest itself in many ways: fear of losing money, fear of making the wrong decision, fear of missing an opportunity, or fear of seeing a winning trade turn into a loss. When fear takes over a trader, it can paralyze him, leading him to avoid making necessary decisions, such as closing a losing position or entering a trade that meets all of his criteria. It can also lead to hasty and ill-informed decisions, simply to relieve the anxiety caused by uncertainty. Instead of acting strategically, the trader acts driven by the desire to protect himself from potential pain, often resulting in costly mistakes.

Greed is another emotion that can easily get out of control in trading. When the markets move in a trader's favor and profits start to accumulate, it is easy to get carried away with the euphoria and want more. Greed leads traders to keep positions open for longer than they should, in the hope of making even bigger profits. However, markets are volatile and can change quickly. What seemed like a winning trade can turn into a loss if the trader does not know when to exit. Greed can also lead traders to increase their risk exposure, opening more positions or investing more capital than they can afford, in search of a quick profit. This lack of control can result in devastating losses when the market inevitably moves against you.

Panic is another emotional state that can arise when a trade goes wrong. When prices start moving in the opposite direction than expected, it is natural to feel a wave of panic. In this state, the trader may go into survival mode, making impulsive decisions to cut losses as quickly as possible, without considering whether those decisions are actually the best in the long term. Panic can lead to selling at the worst time, just before the market reverses, or closing a winning position too soon for fear that profits will evaporate. The result is that, instead of managing the situation calmly and strategically, the trader acts irrationally, amplifying their losses or reducing their potential profits.

Euphoria, although it seems like a positive emotion, can also be dangerous. After a series of successful trades, a trader may feel invincible, believing that he has dominated the market. This feeling of euphoria can lead to complacency, where the trader begins to ignore his own trading rules, takes unnecessary risks and becomes overconfident in his own abilities. Euphoria can cloud judgment, causing the trader to underestimate risks and overestimate opportunities, which can lead to costly mistakes. It is in these moments of euphoria that many traders make their most serious mistakes, believing that the market will always move in their favor.

Hope is another emotion that can work against the trader. When a trade goes against expectations, it is easy to cling to the hope that the market will turn around and the position will become profitable again. This hope can lead to holding losing positions for too long, accumulating larger and larger losses. Instead of accepting the reality that the trade is not working and closing it to limit losses, the trader clings to the illusion that things will get better, which rarely happens. Hope, when not backed by a solid strategy, can be a path to ruin.

The solution to uncontrolled emotions in trading is not to eliminate them, because that is impossible. We are human beings, not machines, and emotions are a natural part of our experience. However, it is crucial to learn how to manage them and not allow them to dominate our trading decisions. The key is to develop a disciplined mindset, where every decision is made based on a clear and well-thought-out trading plan, not in response to the emotions of the moment.

An effective way to manage emotions is through the practice of patience. Instead of reacting immediately to every market move, it is important to take the time to calmly evaluate the situation. This may include waiting for a signal to be confirmed before entering a trade, or resisting the temptation to close a winning position early for fear of the market turning against you. Patience allows decisions to be made logically and strategically, rather than being driven by fear or greed.

Another important tool is to keep a trading journal. Documenting each operation, along with the emotions felt during the process, can help identify emotional patterns that lead to errors. Over time, this self-reflection exercise can help traders recognize when they are acting under the influence of uncontrolled emotions and take steps to correct their behavior before it causes damage. A trading journal also provides an objective record of what works and what doesn't, which can help reinforce decisions based on logic and strategy, rather than emotion.

Finally, it is essential to remember that trading is a long-term game. No matter how tempting it is to get carried away by the emotions of the moment, it's important to maintain perspective and remember that each trade is just one part of a bigger picture. Losing a trade does not mean you are failing, and winning a trade does not mean you have dominated the market. By maintaining this perspective, traders can better manage their emotions and make decisions that benefit them in the long term, rather than getting carried away by the emotional swings of the markets.

In short, uncontrolled emotions are one of the main causes of errors in trading. Fear, greed, panic, euphoria and hope, when not managed properly, can lead to impulsive and ill-informed decisions. However, with a disciplined mindset, patience, self-reflection, and a long-term view, it is possible to keep emotions in check and operate more effectively. By doing so, traders not only improve their results, but also enjoy a more balanced and less stressful trading experience.

Over-opening of Operations

Over-opening trades is a common mistake among traders, especially those who are new to the markets or who feel overconfident after a few successful trades. This mistake involves opening too many trades at the same time, without properly considering the risks involved or the ability to manage so many positions effectively. Although it may seem that the more trades opened, the greater the opportunities to make money, the reality is that over-opening trades can lead to a rapid and uncontrolled collapse of a trader's portfolio.

When a trader opens multiple trades simultaneously, they are dividing their attention and resources. Each trade requires careful monitoring as markets can change quickly and it is essential to stay aware of how open positions are performing. However, when there are too many operations in play, it is easy to lose control, not know which one to prioritize, and end up making hasty or ill-informed decisions. Lack of focus and information overload can lead to the trader feeling overwhelmed, increasing the risk of making serious mistakes.

Another problem with over-opening operations is the lack of capital to properly manage risk. Each trade opened requires a certain amount of capital, and when too many positions are opened, the capital is dispersed, leaving less room to handle each trade properly. This can lead to situations where the trader does not have enough capital to cover losses if the market moves against him, or is forced to close positions prematurely because he cannot keep them all open at the same time. The result is greater exposure to risk and a greater likelihood of suffering significant losses.

Over-opening can also affect the trader's psychology. With so many trades open, it is easy to feel nervous or anxious, especially when positions are not performing as expected. The trader may feel trapped, unable to make rational decisions because there are too many variables to consider at the same time. This anxiety can lead to impulsive decisions, such as closing winning trades too early for fear of missing out on profits, or holding losing positions in the hope that they will reverse, all in an attempt to reduce stress.

Furthermore, when a trader has too many open trades, it is difficult to keep detailed and exhaustive track of each one. Carefully analyzing market conditions, evaluating charts, and following relevant news are tasks that require time and concentration. With multiple active trades, these tasks become even more challenging, and it is easy to overlook important details that could make the difference between a winning trade and a losing one. This lack of monitoring can result in the accumulation of small losses that, together, can have a significant impact on the portfolio.

The lack of a clear focus is also a risk associated with over-opening operations. When a trader opens too many positions, he often does so without a well-defined strategy, simply because he sees multiple opportunities and does not want to miss any. However, this lack of focus can lead to a disorganized portfolio, where holdings are poorly aligned with each other, which can amplify overall risk. For example, if all trades are linked to the same sector or currency, any adverse change in that sector or currency can negatively affect all positions at once, multiplying losses.

Another important aspect is time management. Successful trading requires efficient time management, and over-opening trades can make this extremely difficult. With so many positions open, the trader may find himself jumping from one to another without being able to dedicate enough time to any of them. This not only impacts the ability to make informed decisions, but can also lead to mental and physical exhaustion, which in turn reduces the ability to think clearly and make strategic decisions.

It is crucial to understand that in trading, more is not always better. The quality of operations is much more important than the quantity. A trader who focuses on a few well-planned and managed trades has a greater chance of success than one who spreads himself across too many positions simultaneously. By limiting the number of open trades, the trader can concentrate better, manage risk more effectively and make more informed decisions.

To avoid over-opening trades, it is important for the trader to have a clear trading plan that defines how many positions they can effectively handle at any given time. This plan must take into account the available capital, the ability to manage risk and the time that the trader can dedicate to monitoring each operation. It is also helpful to set personal limits, such as a maximum number of trades open at one time, and adhere to these limits in a disciplined manner.

In short, over-opening trades is a mistake that can have serious consequences for any trader. Opening too many positions at the same time disperses attention, increases risk and can lead to impulsive and ill-informed decisions. In addition, it makes it difficult to properly monitor each operation and can generate unnecessary stress that affects the trader's psychology. To operate successfully, it is essential to prioritize quality over quantity, manage risk effectively and maintain a clear and disciplined approach. By doing so, traders can reduce the likelihood of making costly mistakes and increase their chances of long-term success in the markets.

Adrianne Morel

Negligence in Risk Management

Negligence in risk management is one of the most common and dangerous mistakes a trader can make. In the world of trading, risk is an inevitable part of every trade. No matter how confident you are in an investment or how favorable the market seems, there is always a chance that things will not go as expected. This is where risk management comes into play. This process involves identifying, evaluating and taking measures to minimize potential losses in each transaction. Without proper management, a single adverse market move can erase days, weeks or even months of gains in a matter of minutes.

One of the biggest mistakes traders make when they neglect risk management is not setting a clear limit for their losses. This limit, known as a stop loss, is an essential tool that allows traders to control how much they are willing to lose on a trade before closing it. Without a stop loss, it is easy to get carried away hoping that the market will turn around and that losses will be recovered. But the market does not always follow the trader's wishes, and what could have been a small, controlled loss turns into a devastating loss that affects the entire portfolio. Ignoring the use of a stop loss is like driving without brakes, trusting that the road will always be straight and clear of obstacles.

Another critical aspect of risk management that is often overlooked is diversification. Many traders make the mistake of putting too much capital into a single trade or a single asset, hoping that this investment will generate large profits. Although concentrating resources on a single opportunity may seem like a good strategy in a favorable market, it actually increases risk significantly. If that particular trade or asset does not perform as expected, the negative impact on the trader's portfolio will be much greater. Diversification, on the other hand, allows risk to be spread across different assets or markets, so that losses in one area can be offset by gains in another. It is a strategy that reduces vulnerability to unforeseen events and helps protect capital in the long term.

Lack of understanding of leverage is another way traders can be negligent in risk management. Leverage allows traders to trade with more money than they actually have in their account, which can increase both profits and losses. Although leverage may seem like a powerful tool for multiplying profits, it also amplifies risk proportionately. Many novice traders fall into the trap of using excessive leverage without fully understanding the consequences. When the market moves against you, losses multiply quickly, and before the trader knows it, they may find themselves in significant debt. The use of leverage should be handled with extreme caution and always in the context of a well-planned risk management strategy.

Another common mistake related to negligence in risk management is failure to monitor and adjust open positions. Once a trade is underway, many traders tend to forget about it, trusting that the market will behave as they predicted. However, financial markets are dynamic and can change rapidly due to a variety of factors, such as economic news, geopolitical events, or changes in supply and demand. It is vital that traders monitor their positions regularly and are willing to adjust their strategy if market conditions change. This may involve moving the stop loss, closing a position early, or reducing exposure in a volatile market. Lack of follow-through can lead to unpleasant surprises, such as a trade that suddenly becomes a huge loss because the trader did not act in time.

Furthermore, risk management not only applies to each individual trade, but also to the trading strategy as a whole. A common mistake is not having a clear view of how risk is being managed in the context of the entire portfolio. A trader may be managing risk well on individual trades, but if he does not have a coherent risk strategy for his entire portfolio, he could still be exposed to significant losses. For example, if all operations are related to the same sector or asset, the overall risk of the portfolio is much higher, because any adverse change in that sector or asset will affect all positions at the same time. It is important for traders to evaluate how each trade affects their overall risk exposure and make decisions that keep their portfolio balanced and protected.

Negligence in risk management can also be fueled by a lack of discipline. It's easy, especially after a streak of successful trading, to relax and start taking shortcuts. Traders may stop following their own risk management rules, believing that they are in control and that the market will continue in their favor. However, this lack of discipline can be costly. The market is unpredictable, and the lack of consistent and rigorous risk management can quickly lead to significant losses. Discipline in the application of risk management rules is essential to maintain consistency and long-term profitability.

In short, negligence in risk management is a mistake that can have devastating consequences for traders. Whether it's not using a stop loss, not diversifying properly, misunderstanding leverage, not tracking positions, or simply a lack of discipline, a lack of attention to risk management puts capital and success at risk. long term. Risk management is not an optional aspect of trading; It is an essential part of every decision a trader makes. By adopting a sound risk management strategy and following it rigorously, traders can protect their capital, reduce the impact of losses, and increase their chances of success in the financial markets.

The Myth of Easy Money

The myth of easy money is one of the most seductive and dangerous traps that a trader can fall into, especially those who are starting out in the world of trading. This myth is the mistaken belief that trading is a quick and easy way to make money, that with a few successful trades you can achieve wealth almost instantly. It is a mirage that attracts many with promises of financial freedom and huge profits with minimal effort. However, the reality is very different. Trading is a discipline that requires time, patience, study and careful risk management. Believing in the myth of easy money is not only an illusion, but it can also lead to catastrophic financial decisions.

One of the reasons this myth is so appealing is the way trading is presented on many platforms and advertisements. It is common to see success stories of traders who have apparently made large sums of money in a short time. These stories are often accompanied by images of luxury cars, mansions and exotic vacations, all to give the impression that trading is the key to a life of effortless opulence. But what isn't shown is the hard work, the long hours of study, the losses those traders have faced, and the time it has taken them to develop the skills necessary to succeed. These success stories often fail to mention that the path to trading success is full of challenges, failures, and lessons learned through experience.

The myth of easy money is also fueled by the exciting and fast nature of trading. Financial markets can change in a matter of seconds, and it is possible to see the value of an investment rise or fall dramatically in a short time. This speed and dynamism may give the impression that it is easy to make money quickly, but what you don't see is the volatility and risk that come with these rapid moves. A trader who gets carried away by emotion and the hope of quick profits can find himself on an emotional roller coaster, with peaks of euphoria when things are going well and abysmal drops when the market moves against him. This type of approach is not sustainable in the long term and can lead to impulsive decisions that result in large losses.

Furthermore, the belief in easy money often leads traders to take unnecessary risks. When someone believes that it is easy to make money in trading, they are more likely to invest large sums of money without a clear strategy, relying on luck or intuition rather than informed analysis. This type of behavior is dangerous because it ignores the basic principles of risk management, which are essential to protect capital in an environment as uncertain as financial markets. Without a solid strategy and a clear understanding of the risks involved, losses can quickly accumulate, and the dream of easy money turns into a financial nightmare.

Another aspect of the easy money myth is the lack of education and preparation. Many novice traders jump into the market without taking the time to learn the fundamentals of trading, understand how the markets work, or develop a trading plan. Instead of investing in their education, they trust that they will be able to learn as they go or that luck will be on their side. This approach is very dangerous, because trading is not a game of chance. It requires in-depth knowledge of the markets, an understanding of investment strategies, and the ability to analyze and make data-driven decisions. Without this preparation, it is almost impossible to have long-term success in trading, and the belief in easy money only leads to disappointment and financial loss.

The myth of easy money can also cause traders to underestimate the importance of patience and discipline. Successful trading is not about making large sums of money in a short time, but about building profits consistently over time. This requires patience to wait for the right opportunities and discipline to follow a trading plan even when things don't go as planned. Traders looking for easy money often jump from trade to trade, trying to chase quick profits, rather than building a solid strategy and sticking to it. This lack of focus and a long-term strategy can lead to an endless cycle of profits and losses, without achieving real growth in the portfolio.

It is also important to understand that financial markets are unpredictable and influenced by a multitude of factors that are outside the control of any trader. Even the most experienced and educated traders face losses, and it is part of the process of learning and improving at trading. Believing in the myth of easy money can lead to the false expectation that each trade will be successful, and when things do not go as expected, the trader can feel frustrated, demotivated, or even blame the market instead of reflecting on their own decisions. and strategies. This type of mentality is counterproductive and can prevent the trader from learning from his mistakes and improving over time.

To combat the myth of easy money, it is essential that traders adopt a realistic mindset and are willing to invest time and effort in their education and development. Successful trading is a marathon, not a sprint. It requires dedication, continuous learning, and the willingness to face and overcome challenges. Traders should focus on developing skills and strategies that allow them to trade effectively and manage risks appropriately. Only then will they be able to build a sustainable path to trading success, instead of falling into the trap of easy money.

In conclusion, the myth of easy money is a dangerous illusion that can lead traders to make reckless decisions and risk their capital without proper preparation. Trading is a discipline that requires education, patience, discipline and careful risk management. Those looking for quick and easy profits often end up disappointed and with big losses. Instead of chasing a pipe dream, it is crucial that traders take a realistic approach and are willing to work hard to develop the skills and strategies necessary for long-term success in the financial markets. Only then can they avoid the pitfalls of the easy money myth and build a solid foundation for their financial future.

Lack of Education and Knowledge

Lack of education and knowledge is one of the most serious and common mistakes that traders can make when starting their path in the world of trading. This error manifests itself when a person enters the financial markets without having dedicated enough time to learn the fundamentals of trading, the basic strategies, and the risks involved. It's like trying to navigate a boat without knowing how to handle the rudder or the sails. Although trading may seem simple from the outside, with up and down charts and the promise of quick profits, the reality is that the markets are complex and full of nuances that can only be understood with proper education and in-depth knowledge.

One of the most common problems related to lack of education is that many novice traders underestimate the importance of learning before starting to trade real money. It's easy to get carried away with the initial enthusiasm, especially when you see others succeed or when the markets seem to be in an unstoppable uptrend. But what these traders don't see is the time and effort that others have invested in their training. Trading is not something that can be mastered in a few days or weeks; It requires constant learning and a willingness to study, practice, and adapt as experience is gained. Without a solid foundation of knowledge, traders risk making decisions based on assumptions, hunches or misinformation, which inevitably leads to losses.

Lack of education can also lead to serious misunderstandings about how financial markets work. For example, many novice traders do not fully understand key concepts such as volatility, leverage, or the importance of technical and fundamental indicators. Volatility refers to fluctuations in asset prices, and is a crucial aspect to consider when trading. Without understanding how to handle volatility, a trader can get caught up in sharp market movements that can result in large losses. Likewise, leverage, which allows traders to trade with more money than they actually have, may seem like a quick way to increase profits, but without the proper knowledge, it can amplify losses in devastating ways. Technical and fundamental indicators are essential tools for analyzing the market and making informed decisions, and not knowing or ignoring them can leave traders trading blind.

Another consequence of lack of education is the tendency to trust unreliable sources of information or advice from other traders without critical evaluation. The Internet is full of websites, forums, and gurus promising foolproof strategies or secrets to make quick money in trading. Without the knowledge to discern what information is valuable and what is misleading, traders can easily fall into traps or follow strategies that are not appropriate for their risk profile or market conditions. Not only can this lead to financial losses, but it can also lead to confusion and disappointment, as the trader does not understand why their trades are not working as they expected. Trading education includes learning to filter and evaluate information, and developing a critical approach that allows you to make decisions based on data and analysis rather than emotion or third-party advice.

Furthermore, lack of knowledge also affects the trader's ability to manage risk effectively. Trading involves inherent risks, and part of being a successful trader is knowing how to minimize those risks. Without a clear understanding of risk management tools and techniques, traders can expose themselves to losses that could have been avoided. For example, not knowing how to set a stop loss, which is an automatic limit to close a trade when the market moves against it, can result in a much larger loss than the trader was willing to take. Risk management is not only an important part of trading, it is essential for survival in the markets. Lack of education in this area can be the difference between a trader who is able to recover from a bad streak and one who loses all of his capital in a series of bad decisions.

Another critical aspect that is affected by lack of education is the psychology of trading. The market not only tests a trader's technical knowledge, but also his ability to manage his emotions under pressure. Fear, greed, euphoria, and despair are emotions that all traders experience at some point, and without an understanding of how to manage them, these emotions can lead to impulsive and costly decisions. Trading education includes learning about market psychology and how to stay calm and disciplined even when things don't go as planned. A trader who understands how emotions work in trading will be better prepared to make rational decisions and avoid the mistakes that can result from reacting emotionally to market movements.

Finally, lack of education and knowledge also prevents traders from developing an effective trading plan. A trading plan is a roadmap that guides all trading decisions, from when to enter and exit the market to how to manage risk and how to evaluate past trades. Without the necessary knowledge, many traders trade without a clear plan, leaving them at the mercy of market fluctuations and their own emotions. A well-designed trading plan is based on a deep understanding of the market, trading strategies and the trader's personal objectives. Without this planning, trading becomes a series of random bets, rather than a strategic, controlled approach to generating long-term profits.

In conclusion, lack of education and knowledge is a major obstacle that can prevent traders from achieving success in the financial markets. Trading is not an activity that can be mastered without effort or preparation; It requires a constant commitment to learning and skill development. Those who attempt to trade without proper education are exposed to unnecessary risks, financial losses, and a limited understanding of how the markets really work. To overcome this challenge, it is essential that traders invest time and resources in their education, seek out reliable sources of information, take the time to learn and practice, and be willing to adapt and improve as they gain experience. Only with solid knowledge and continued education is it possible to successfully navigate the complex and volatile financial markets.

Ignore Market Trends

Ignoring market trends is one of the most common and costly mistakes traders can make. Market trends are directional patterns that show how asset prices are moving over time, and can be up, down, or sideways. Understanding and following these trends is crucial to making informed and effective trading decisions. However, many traders, especially those who are new to trading, often underestimate the importance of trends or simply ignore them completely, relying on their intuition or short-term price movements that can be misleading.

When a trader ignores market trends, they run the risk of trading against the general direction in which the market is moving. This is a mistake that can result in significant losses because trading against the trend is like swimming against the current: you may make some progress, but eventually the power of the current will sweep you away. Trends exist because they reflect the collective strength of the market, driven by the sum of all the buying and selling decisions that market participants are making. When the market is in an uptrend, it means that most traders and investors are buying, which causes prices to rise. Likewise, a downtrend indicates that the majority are selling, which causes prices to drop. Going against these forces is risky and can lead to rapid and deep losses.

One of the problems that arises from ignoring trends is that traders can get caught up in short-term price movements that do not reflect the true direction of the market. It is easy to get carried away by small spikes or drops in the price of an asset and think that they represent a new trend, when in reality they are just temporary fluctuations. Without a clear understanding of the overall trend, traders can enter and exit the market at the wrong times, buying when they should be selling or selling when they should be buying. These types of errors not only result in losses, but can also lead to frustration and confusion, as the trader does not understand why their trades are not working.

Another important aspect of following market trends is that it helps traders better manage risk. When a trader trades in favor of the trend, he is aligning his decisions with the general direction of the market, which tends to reduce the risk of losses. This does not mean that trading with the trend guarantees profits, but it does mean that the trader is making decisions based on analysis of the dominant direction of the market, which is generally a safer strategy than trading against that direction. Ignoring the trend, on the other hand, increases risk because the trader is betting against the collective strength of the market, which is harder to predict and control.

The market trend also provides useful context for interpreting other technical and fundamental indicators. Many traders use tools such as moving averages, momentum indicators, and chart patterns to make trading decisions. However, these indicators are much more effective when interpreted within the context of the overall market trend. For example, a buy signal generated by a technical indicator will be more reliable if it is aligned with an uptrend. Ignoring the trend and relying solely on an indicator can lead to false signals and erroneous trading decisions. Traders who understand the trend can use these indicators to confirm their analyzes and increase the probability of success in their trades.

Furthermore, ignoring market trends can negatively affect the trader's psychology. Trading against the trend can be emotionally draining because it goes against the mainstream of the market. Traders who insist on trading against the trend may find themselves trapped in a cycle of losses, which can lead to feelings of frustration, despair, and eventually making impulsive decisions. On the other hand, trading with the trend tends to be less stressful and more rewarding, since the trader is following the natural direction of the market and is more likely to see positive results. Confidence in the trend can help you maintain calm and discipline, which is essential for long-term success in trading.

One of the reasons why some traders ignore trends is the belief that they can predict market reversal points, that is, the exact moment when a trend will change direction. This is an extremely difficult task, even for the most experienced traders, because markets are unpredictable and influenced by a large number of external factors. Trying to predict a trend reversal is risky and often results in losses as it is almost impossible to determine precisely when that reversal will occur. Instead of trying to predict reversals, it is more prudent to follow the current trend until there are clear signs that it is changing. This not only reduces risk but also increases the likelihood of capturing significant market moves.

Another common mistake associated with ignoring market trends is failure to adapt to changing market conditions. Markets are not static; Trends can change over time and it is important for traders to be flexible and willing to adjust their strategies as necessary. Ignoring a new trend because one is clinging to an old view of the market can lead to losses, as the trader is falling behind the current reality of the market. Successful traders are those who can recognize when a trend is changing and quickly adapt to new conditions. This requires constant market monitoring, as well as a willingness to review and adjust the trading plan as necessary.

Finally, it is important to note that following the market trend does not mean operating without a plan or strategy. In fact, it is quite the opposite. Trend-following traders must have a clear plan that includes how to identify a trend, when to enter and exit the market, and how to manage risk in the process. This structured approach allows the trader to take full advantage of the opportunities the market offers while minimizing the risk of loss. Ignoring the trend and trading without a solid plan is a recipe for failure, as it leaves the trader vulnerable to unpredictable market fluctuations and impulsive decisions.

In conclusion, ignoring market trends is a serious mistake that can lead to significant losses and a frustrating trading experience. Trends reflect the general direction of the market and offer valuable guidance for making informed and confident trading decisions. By following the trend, traders can align themselves with market strength, better manage risk, and increase their chances of success. Ignoring the trend, on the other hand, is risky and can lead to erroneous trading decisions based on incorrect assumptions or temporary market fluctuations. To avoid this mistake, it is crucial that traders learn to identify and follow market trends, and are willing to adapt to changing market conditions to maintain their competitive advantage.

Excessive Confidence in Technical Indicators

Overreliance on technical indicators is a common mistake among many traders, especially those who are new to the world of trading. Technical indicators are popular tools that help analyze the market by providing signals about possible price movements. These tools include moving averages, the relative strength index (RSI), the MACD, and many others. However, while technical indicators can be helpful in making informed decisions, relying too much on them without considering other factors can lead to erroneous decisions and significant losses.

One of the fundamental problems with relying excessively on technical indicators is that they do not always reflect the full reality of the market. Technical indicators are based on historical data, that is, what has already happened in the market. They use mathematical formulas to interpret this data and generate signals that suggest possible future trends. However, the market is influenced by a wide variety of factors, including economic events, news, political decisions and changes in investor perception. These factors can cause sudden and sharp movements that technical indicators cannot predict. Therefore, a trader who blindly trusts a technical indicator without taking into account the overall market context could find himself caught in unexpected movements that result in losses.

Another problem with overreliance on technical indicators is the tendency to overinterpret the signals they generate. Many traders, especially those who are new, can fall into the trap of viewing each indicator signal as a guarantee that the market will move in the suggested direction. This can lead to impulsive decisions, such as entering or exiting the market at the wrong time. Technical indicators are not infallible and can often generate false or contradictory signals. For example, one indicator may suggest a buy, while another could indicate a sell. Relying too much on these indicators without considering the overall market situation and without using other analysis methods can lead to wrong decisions resulting in losses.

Additionally, overuse of technical indicators can lead to analysis paralysis. This is a phenomenon where a trader feels overwhelmed by the amount of information provided by the indicators and as a result has difficulty making a decision. Some traders use multiple indicators at the same time in hopes of getting a clearer view of the market. However, this often results in conflicting signals and further confusion. Instead of helping, too many indicators can hinder decision-making and cause the trader to miss valuable opportunities or, worse yet, make decisions based on conflicting information. In trading, less is often more. Rather than relying on a multitude of indicators, it is more effective to use a few key indicators that complement each other and are well understood.

A crucial aspect that many traders overlook by relying too much on technical indicators is the lack of adaptation to changing market conditions. Financial markets are dynamic and can change rapidly due to a variety of factors, such as unexpected news or changes in economic policy. Technical indicators, being based on past data, cannot always adapt to these changes quickly and effectively. A trader who relies too much on these indicators may continue to trade based on the signals he receives, without realizing that market conditions have changed. This can lead to significant losses, as decisions are based on outdated information that is no longer relevant to the current market situation.

Another common mistake related to overreliance on technical indicators is using them without really understanding how they work. It is easy for a trader to fall into the trap of simply following the signals that indicators generate without taking the time to understand the formulas and principles behind them. Each indicator has its own limitations and is designed to work in certain market conditions. For example, some indicators are more effective in trending markets, while others work better in sideways markets or without a clear trend. Without a solid understanding of how and when to use each indicator, traders risk misinterpreting signals and making poor decisions that result in losses. Education is key; Traders should take the time to learn how technical indicators work, their limitations, and how to integrate them into a broader trading strategy.

Additionally, it is important to remember that technical indicators are just one tool in the trader's arsenal, and should not be used as the sole basis for making decisions. Successful trading requires a holistic view that combines different analysis methods, such as fundamental analysis, reading news and economic events, and observing price action. Fundamental analysis, for example, can provide deeper insight into the health of a company or economy, which can influence long-term market direction. While technical analysis focuses on short-term price movements, fundamental analysis can help identify more sustainable trends. Ignoring these other methods of analysis in favor of technical indicators can lead to an incomplete understanding of the market and trading decisions that are not supported by a solid foundation.

Finally, relying too much on technical indicators can also negatively affect the trader's psychology. Overreliance on technical signals can create a false sense of security, which can lead to reduced discipline and increased risk-taking. Traders may be tempted to increase their position size or hold a trade longer than they should because they trust the technical indicator to guide them in the right direction. However, when the market moves against the technical signal, these traders may find themselves in a difficult situation, trapped in a losing trade that should have been closed earlier. Trading psychology is a crucial part of success, and relying too much on technical indicators can erode discipline and the ability to make rational decisions under pressure.

In conclusion, excessive reliance on technical indicators is a mistake that can lead to erroneous trading decisions and financial losses. Although technical indicators are valuable tools for analyzing the market, they should not be the only basis for making trading decisions. Financial markets are complex and influenced by a variety of factors that technical indicators cannot always capture. To avoid this mistake, traders should use technical indicators as one part of a broader trading strategy that includes fundamental analysis, observation of price action, and a clear understanding of current market conditions. By doing so, traders can make more informed decisions and increase their chances of trading success.

Adrianne Morel

Operating without Understanding the Economic Context

Trading without understanding the economic context is one of the most dangerous mistakes a trader can make. The financial market does not operate in a vacuum; It is deeply influenced by a wide range of economic factors that can significantly affect price behavior. These factors include monetary policies, government decisions, economic indicators, global events, and changes in interest rates, among others. When a trader does not take the economic context into account when making trading decisions, they run the risk of making trades that are not aligned with the reality of the market, which can lead to significant losses.

The economic context is essential because it provides the framework in which asset prices move. For example, when a central bank announces a change in interest rates, this can have a direct impact on the value of that country's currency. If a trader is trading in the foreign exchange (Forex) market without being aware of these decisions, he could find himself on the wrong side of a trade, suffering significant losses due to sudden movements in the market that he did not anticipate. Similarly, reports on gross domestic product (GDP), inflation, and unemployment are key indicators that can influence the stock market. Ignoring these reports or not understanding their meaning can lead to ill-informed decisions resulting in losses.

Trading without understanding the economic context also means that a trader may not be prepared to handle the volatility that these events can generate. Markets can react sharply and sometimes irrationally to important economic news. Without a proper understanding of the context, a trader can enter the market just before an important announcement, without being aware that the risk of volatility is high. This can lead to situations where the market moves quickly against the trader's position, leaving them with little time to react. In these cases, a lack of preparation and understanding of the economic environment can result in rapid and severe losses.

Another critical aspect is that trading without understanding the economic context can lead to unrealistic expectations about the market. A trader who is not informed about the state of the global or local economy may enter the market with the expectation that prices will move in a certain way, based solely on technical analysis or intuition. However, the reality is that asset prices are influenced by a combination of technical and economic factors. If a trader does not take economic factors into account, it is likely that his expectations will not align with market reality, which can lead to poor trading decisions. For example, during an economic recession, stock prices are likely to fall, and a trader who is unaware of this situation could enter a long position (betting that prices will rise) at a time when the market is destined to fall.

Furthermore, the economic context also affects the perception of risk and reward in the market. In times of economic uncertainty, investors tend to be more cautious, and prices of assets considered riskier, such as emerging company stocks or developing market currencies, may fall. On the other hand, in times of economic growth, investors may be more optimistic and willing to take on more risk, which may lead to an increase in the prices of these assets. A trader who does not understand this context could misinterpret market signals, assuming that a drop in prices is a buying opportunity, when in fact it is a sign that the market is in risk aversion mode. Similarly, he might mistake a rise in prices as a sign that the market is in an uptrend, without realizing that it is a temporary rally in a bear market.

Understanding the economic context is also crucial to managing risk effectively. An informed trader is better able to anticipate events that could negatively impact their trades and can therefore take steps to protect themselves, such as adjusting the size of their positions or setting tighter stop-loss orders. On the other hand, a trader who ignores the economic context may be trading with an unnecessarily high level of risk, since he is not considering external factors that could affect the outcome of his trades. Risk management is a fundamental part of trading, and without a proper understanding of the economic environment, a trader is trading blind, which increases the likelihood of experiencing significant losses.

Furthermore, trading without understanding the economic context can also lead to a lack of confidence in trading decisions. Traders who do not have a clear understanding of the environment in which they are trading may doubt their decisions or feel unsure about when to enter or exit the market. This lack of confidence can lead to a series of mistakes, such as exiting a winning trade too soon, holding a losing trade for too long, or avoiding making important decisions for fear of making a mistake. On the contrary, traders who are well informed about the economic context are more likely to make safer decisions and follow their trading plans with discipline.

In the long term, trading without understanding the economic context can limit a trader's success. Markets are complex and influenced by a multitude of constantly changing factors. A trader who does not make an effort to stay informed about these factors is limiting his ability to adapt to changing market conditions.

Success in trading is not only based on technical skill, but also on the ability to understand the broader environment in which decisions are being made. Those traders who take the time to educate themselves about the economic context, read economic reports, and follow relevant news are better able to identify opportunities and avoid unnecessary risks.

In conclusion, trading without understanding the economic context is a serious mistake that can have significant negative consequences on trading results. The economic context provides the framework within which markets move, and without a proper understanding of this environment, traders run the risk of making ill-informed decisions, poorly managing risk, and having unrealistic expectations about the market. To avoid this mistake, it is crucial that traders stay informed about the economic factors affecting the market, consider these factors in their trading decisions, and adapt their strategies based on the economic environment. By doing so, traders can improve their ability to make informed decisions, manage risk effectively, and increase their chances of success in the financial market.

Trade with Capital You Can't Lose

Trading with capital that you cannot lose is one of the most dangerous mistakes a trader can make. When we talk about capital in trading, we are referring to the money that a trader allocates to invest in the financial markets with the hope of obtaining a profit. However, not all money should be used for trading, especially if that money is essential for daily living, to cover basic expenses, or to meet important financial obligations. Trading with money you cannot afford to lose not only puts your financial stability at risk, but can also negatively affect your mental and emotional health, leading to hasty and irrational decisions.

The first reason why trading with capital you can't lose is such a serious mistake is because it adds unnecessary emotional pressure. Trading is already a stressful activity, as markets can be volatile and prices can fluctuate unpredictably. When a trader uses money they cannot afford to lose, the fear of losing that money becomes overwhelming. This fear can cloud the trader's judgment, leading them to make impulsive decisions in a desperate attempt to avoid losses. For example, a trader might close a trade prematurely for fear that the market will move against him, even if the fundamentals indicate that the trade could be profitable in the long term. Similarly, the same fear could lead a trader to hold a losing position in the hope that the market will recover, often resulting in even larger losses.

Additionally, trading with capital that you cannot lose can lead to excessive risk taking. When a trader is trading with money that he needs to cover essential expenses, he may be tempted to take on more risk than he would normally take in an attempt to make quick profits. This "all or nothing" mentality is extremely dangerous in trading, as markets do not always behave in predictable ways. Even if a trade looks promising, there is always a chance that the market could move against it, which could result in a significant loss. When trading with money you cannot afford to lose, any loss can have devastating consequences for your financial life, which could lead to problems such as debt, difficulty paying bills, or even the loss of important assets.

Another problem that arises when trading with capital that you cannot lose is the lack of objectivity. Successful traders are those who can make decisions based on careful and rational analysis, rather than being carried away by emotions. However, when the money at stake is essential to your financial well-being, it is much more difficult to remain objective. Every market move can feel like a direct threat to your financial security, which can cause you to overreact to market fluctuations. This lack of objectivity can lead to a number of mistakes, such as entering into impulsive trades, ignoring warning signs, or overanalyzing every market move in an attempt to avoid losses. Ultimately, a lack of objectivity can result in inconsistent and often costly trading decisions.

Additionally, trading with capital you can't lose can have a lasting impact on your relationship with trading and with money in general. Financial losses can be extremely difficult to handle, especially if those losses affect your ability to live comfortably or meet your financial obligations. The pain and stress associated with losing essential money can lead to a cycle of guilt, regret, and fear that can affect your ability to make rational decisions in the future. Some traders, after experiencing significant losses with money they could not afford to lose, develop a risk aversion that makes them unable to trade effectively again. Others may fall into the trap of trying to recoup their losses by trading more aggressively, which often leads to more losses.

An additional consequence of trading with capital that you cannot lose is the impact on your personal life and relationships. Financial stress can affect all areas of your life, from your mental health to your relationships with family and friends. When financial losses accumulate, conflicts can arise in the home, especially if the money lost was necessary to cover common expenses such as rent, mortgages, children's education, or daily needs. The tension and stress resulting from these losses can lead to arguments, resentment, and in some cases, relationship breakdowns. Additionally, constant stress can affect your physical health, causing problems such as insomnia, anxiety, and other stress-related conditions.

It is essential to understand that trading must be done with capital that is considered "risk money", that is, money that, if lost, will not affect your quality of life or your financial stability. This risk money should be a separate part of your savings, distinct from funds intended for emergencies, daily expenses, or any other important financial needs. By only trading with money you can afford to lose, you give yourself the freedom to make trading decisions without the emotional weight of knowing that your financial well-being is at stake. This allows you to be more objective, follow your trading plan with discipline, and accept losses as part of the process, rather than seeing them as direct threats to your financial security.

Trading with capital that you can afford to lose also allows you to approach trading with a long-term mindset. Successful trading is not a quick route to wealth, but a process that requires time, patience and careful risk management. When you trade with money you can't afford to lose, it's easy to be tempted to chase quick profits, which often leads to high-risk decisions and, ultimately, losses. Conversely, when you trade with capital you are willing to risk, you can focus on developing and following a solid trading strategy, learning from your mistakes, and improving your skills over time, which increases your chances of long-term success.

In conclusion, trading with capital that you cannot lose is a serious mistake that can have devastating financial, emotional and personal consequences. Trading should be done with risk money, that is, with funds that, if lost, will not affect your financial well-being or quality of life. By avoiding this mistake and only trading with capital you can afford to lose, you can reduce emotional stress, make more objective trading decisions, and maintain a long-term mindset that will help you achieve success in the world of trading. Remember that trading is not a race to quick riches, but a process that requires patience, discipline and careful risk management.

Adrianne Morel

Constantly Change Strategy

Constantly changing strategies is a common mistake that many traders make, especially those who are new to the world of trading. The idea of finding the "perfect strategy" that guarantees consistent profits is attractive, but the reality is that there is no such strategy. Instead of looking for the foolproof strategy, traders should focus on developing a strategy that fits their trading style, financial goals, and risk tolerance. Changing strategies every time something doesn't go as planned is a recipe for frustration and often loss of capital.

The problem with constantly changing strategies is that it prevents a trader from developing the patience and discipline necessary to be successful in trading. Each strategy has its strengths and weaknesses, and you are likely to face ups and downs in its performance. However, when a trader changes strategies at the first sign of difficulty, he never gives the strategy the time necessary to demonstrate its long-term effectiveness. Trading is not a game of instant results; It requires time, analysis and, above all, consistency. Jumping from one strategy to another creates an endless cycle of starting from scratch, making it difficult to progress and learn.

Furthermore, constantly changing strategies can also lead to a lack of confidence in trading decisions. When a trader does not trust his strategy, he is likely to hesitate when making decisions, which can lead to mistakes such as entering or exiting the market at the wrong times. This lack of confidence can also manifest itself in the inability to follow a trading plan with discipline. Without a consistent strategy, traders can make impulsive decisions based on emotions such as fear or greed, rather than based on rational, well-informed analysis. This constant uncertainty is not only mentally exhausting, but can also result in significant financial losses.

Another consequence of constantly changing strategies is the difficulty in evaluating the performance of operations. To determine if a strategy is effective, it is necessary to apply it consistently over a reasonable period of time and under different market conditions. This allows the trader to collect enough data to analyze the strategy's performance, identify patterns, and make adjustments if necessary. However, if a trader changes strategy every time he faces a loss, he will never be able to gather enough information to make an objective evaluation. As a result, he may never know whether a particular strategy could have been profitable in the long term if it had been followed consistently.

Constantly changing strategy can also lead to information overload. Today, there is an overwhelming amount of resources available to traders, from books and courses to seminars and online platforms. While continuing education is important, consuming too much information without clear direction can be counterproductive. Traders who are constantly looking for new strategies may find themselves trapped in an endless learning cycle, where they are constantly searching for the next trading "secret" instead of applying what they already know. This information overload can lead to confusion and the inability to make clear and concise decisions.

Additionally, changing strategies too frequently can incur additional costs that many traders do not consider. Every time a trader adopts a new strategy, he or she may need to invest time and money in learning it, whether through purchasing new resources, performing backtesting, or even subscribing to specific signal services or indicators. . These costs can add up quickly, especially if a trader never commits to a strategy long enough to see a return on their investment. Instead of continually spending on new strategies, it is more efficient and profitable in the long term to spend time perfecting a strategy that is already understood and tested.

Another important issue is that constantly changing strategies can misalign the trader with their objectives and personal style. Each trader is unique, with different goals, risk tolerances, and schedules. Not all strategies are suited to each type of trader, and what works for one may not work for another. For example, a strategy that requires being in front of a screen all day may not be suitable for someone who has a full-time job. Likewise, a strategy that involves high risk may not be suitable for someone with a low tolerance for loss. Constantly changing strategies can lead to a disconnect between trading decisions and personal needs, increasing the risk of making unsustainable decisions in the long term.

Finally, changing strategies too frequently can also impede the development of key trading skills. Successful trading is not only based on the strategy used, but also on the trader's ability to interpret the market, manage risk and maintain discipline. These skills develop over time and with consistent practice. When a trader constantly changes strategies, he is not dedicating the time necessary to develop these fundamental skills. As a result, he may end up relying too much on the strategy itself, rather than his ability to adapt and make informed decisions based on his experience and knowledge of the market.

In conclusion, constantly changing strategies is a mistake that can have negative long-term consequences on a trader's performance. This behavior prevents the development of consistency, patience and discipline, which are essential for trading success. Additionally, it can lead to a lack of confidence in trading decisions, information overload and additional costs, and a disconnect between trading decisions and the trader's personal needs. To avoid this mistake, it is crucial that traders commit to developing and following a strategy that fits their personal style and goals, and give themselves the time to perfect it. By doing so, they will be able to improve their skills, make more informed decisions, and increase their chances of success in the financial market in the long term.

The Mistake of Chasing Losses

Chasing losses is a common and dangerous mistake that many traders make in their quest to recover lost money. This behavior, known in the trading world as "revenge trading," occurs when a trader, after suffering a loss, enters a new trade driven by the desire to quickly recover what was lost, rather than Do it strategically and well thought out. It is an emotional reaction that can lead to a downward spiral of increasing losses, as the trader acts under the influence of fear, anger or frustration, rather than based on a rational analysis of the market.

The first problem with chasing losses is that it often leads to impulsive and poorly informed decisions. After a loss, it's natural to feel disappointed or frustrated. These feelings can cloud a trader's judgment and cause them to enter a new trade without having performed proper analysis. Instead of evaluating the market and waiting for an opportunity with a good chance of success, the trader jumps into the next trade that looks promising, hoping to quickly recover what he lost. These types of hasty trades rarely end well, as they are not based on a solid trading plan, but on the emotional urgency of getting the money back.

Another problem is that chasing losses often leads to increased risk exposure. In his desire to recover what he lost, a trader may begin to make riskier decisions than he would normally make. This may include trading with a larger amount of money, opening larger positions than usual, or entering more volatile markets without a proper understanding of the risks involved. The problem with this approach is that, although it is possible for a trader to get lucky and recover what he lost on a risky trade, those risky trades are much more likely to result in even larger losses. Trading is about managing risk and maximizing the chances of long-term success, but when a trader chases losses, he often ignores these basic principles, leading to a cycle of increasing losses.

Additionally, chasing losses can seriously affect a trader's confidence. Each additional loss can increase feelings of hopelessness and frustration, which in turn can lead to more mistakes. The trader begins to doubt his ability to make correct decisions, and this lack of confidence can result in a negative cycle where losses continue to accumulate. Instead of taking time to reflect on what went wrong, learn from mistakes, and return to the market with a clear mind, the trader feels trapped in a race to recover what was lost, which only serves to deepen the hole in the market. that is found. Trust is essential in trading, and when it is compromised, the trader's performance often suffers as a result.

Another negative aspect of chasing losses is that it can lead to emotional and mental exhaustion. Trading is already a demanding activity, and when you add the emotional burden of trying to recover losses, stress can increase significantly. Traders chasing losses may find themselves trading for long hours, obsessing over every market move and experiencing high levels of anxiety. This state of exhaustion not only affects the ability to make clear decisions, but can also have an impact on other areas of the trader's life, such as health, personal relationships, and general well-being. Trading should be an activity managed with care and balance, but when losses are chased, that balance is quickly lost.

Furthermore, the mistake of chasing losses can become a destructive habit. Once a trader starts revenge trading, it can be difficult to break the cycle. Each loss can trigger a new round of impulsive trading, leading to more losses and more revenge trading. This cycle can continue until the trader has lost a significant portion, if not all, of his capital. For many traders, this cycle only stops when they finally recognize that they have lost more than they can afford and decide to quit trading altogether. It is a downward spiral that could have been avoided if the trader had managed his initial losses more rationally and with a clear strategy.

On the other hand, it is important to understand that losses are an inevitable part of trading. No trader, no matter how experienced, wins every trade. The key to success in trading is not to avoid losses completely, but to manage them effectively. This means accepting losses when they occur, learning from them, and moving forward with discipline and focus. A successful trader knows that a loss does not define his ability or his strategy, but is simply a part of the process. When a trader chases losses, he loses sight of this reality and, instead of learning and improving, he gets carried away by emotions, which almost always leads to more problems.

To avoid the mistake of chasing losses, it is essential that traders have a clear trading plan and follow it with discipline. A trading plan should include specific rules about when to enter and exit a trade, how to manage risk, and how to handle losses. When a trader follows his plan consistently, he is less likely to get carried away by emotions after a loss. It is also helpful to set boundaries to avoid falling into the trap of revenge trading. For example, a trader might decide that after a loss, he will take a break of at least 24 hours before returning to the market. These types of rules can help you maintain focus and avoid impulsive decisions.

In short, chasing losses is a mistake that can have serious consequences for any trader. When trading for revenge, traders get carried away by emotions, make impulsive and risky decisions, and can end up in a downward spiral of increasing losses. This behavior not only affects the trading account, but can also have a negative impact on the trader's confidence, mental health, and overall well-being. To avoid this mistake, it is essential to have a clear trading plan, manage risk effectively and accept losses as a natural part of the trading process. By doing so, traders can avoid falling into the trap of chasing losses and instead focus on developing the patience, discipline, and consistency necessary for long-term success in the market.

Adrianne Morel

Not Keeping a Trading Journal

Not keeping a trading journal is one of the most underrated mistakes, but also one of the most damaging for any trader, regardless of their level of experience. A trading journal is an essential tool that allows traders to keep a detailed record of each of their trades, including aspects such as the reason behind each entry and exit, the results obtained, and the emotions they experienced during the process. However, many traders, especially newbies, underestimate the importance of this habit and end up trading without a clear view of what they are doing right or wrong. The result is that they become susceptible to repeating the same mistakes over and over again, without truly learning from their experiences.

Keeping a trading journal is like having a mirror that shows you exactly what you are doing in the market. Without this mirror, it's easy to fall into the trap of complacency, where you convince yourself that your decisions are always right, even when the results are not. The journal forces you to face the reality of your decisions and results, and provides you with a personal database that you can analyze to identify patterns in your behavior and in the market. For example, you might find that you tend to make hasty decisions when trading after a long day at work, or that your best trades occur when you strictly follow your trading plan. This information is invaluable for improving your performance over time, but you can only obtain it if you keep detailed records of your activities.

Another key benefit of keeping a trading journal is that it helps you maintain discipline. Successful trading relies on consistently following a plan, but discipline can be compromised by emotions, especially after a series of significant losses or gains. When you keep a journal, you force yourself to document every transaction, which adds an additional level of accountability to your decisions. You know that you will have to face your own records, and this may make you think twice before making an impulsive decision. Additionally, the simple act of writing down or recording your thoughts and reasons behind each trade gives you time to reflect, which can often prevent you from making impulsive decisions in the heat of the moment.

Additionally, a trading journal allows you to track your progress over time. Trading is a continuous learning process, and it is not uncommon for traders to forget their past mistakes or achievements they have made. By keeping track of all your trades, you can see how you have evolved, what strategies have worked best for you, and what areas you need to improve. For example, you might notice that over time you have developed better risk management or that you have learned to better control your emotions during periods of high market volatility. This long-term vision is crucial for any trader who aspires to improve and maintain consistent performance over time.

Another important aspect of keeping a trading journal is that it helps you identify patterns in your trading that may not be immediately apparent. Sometimes, a trader may be trading inconsistently without realizing it. For example, you might discover that you tend to hold your winning positions for too short a time and your losing positions for too long. Or you might notice that you tend to trade more aggressively when the market is in an uptrend, but are more conservative in a bear market. These patterns can be difficult to identify without detailed logging, but once you discover them, you can take steps to correct them and improve your overall performance.

Keeping a trading journal is also essential to evaluate the effectiveness of your strategies. Many times, traders try different approaches and tactics, but without proper tracking, it is difficult to know which of them really works and which does not. A journal allows you to keep detailed track of each strategy you use, including the market conditions in which you applied it and the results obtained. Over time, you will be able to see which strategies have been most successful for you and under which market conditions they work best. This information allows you to optimize your approach and focus on what really works, rather than wasting time and resources on tactics that don't deliver consistent results.

Additionally, a trading journal helps you manage your emotions, which are a key factor in success or failure in trading. The market can be an emotionally volatile place, and it's easy to get carried away by fear, greed, or frustration. By documenting your emotions in your journal, you can begin to notice how they influence your trading decisions. For example, you might find that you tend to trade more riskily after a series of losses, or that you are more cautious after a big win. Recognizing these emotional patterns is the first step to controlling them and preventing them from leading you to make irrational decisions that can cost you money.

A trading journal is also useful for reviewing and reflecting after a period of trading. Sometimes, it is necessary to step away from the market and review what you have done from a more objective perspective. By reviewing your journal, you can identify areas where you have made repeated mistakes, as well as areas where you have improved. This reflection is crucial for growth and development as a trader. Additionally, reviewing your journal allows you to remember lessons learned in the past, which helps you avoid making the same mistakes in the future. It is a way to ensure that each trade, whether winning or losing, contributes to your learning and continuous improvement.

Finally, a trading journal can serve as a source of motivation. Trading can be a lonely and challenging journey, and it is easy to feel discouraged after a series of losses or periods of underperformance. However, by reviewing your journal, you can see how much you've progressed, remember your successes, and see the valuable lessons you've learned along the way. This perspective can help you stay motivated and confident, even during difficult times. Knowing that each trade, whether successful or not, is bringing you closer to your long-term goals can be a powerful motivator to keep going and continue improving as a trader.

In short, not keeping a trading journal is a mistake that can cost any trader dearly. Without a detailed record of your trades, it is difficult to learn from your mistakes, identify patterns, evaluate strategies and control your emotions. A trading journal provides you with the clarity and discipline needed to improve your performance over time, and allows you to see your progress tangibly. It is an essential tool for any trader who aspires to be successful in the market, and should not be underestimated. By spending time documenting and analyzing your trades, you can develop a deeper understanding of yourself as a trader, optimize your strategies, and ultimately increase your chances of long-term success in the financial market.

Adrianne Morel

Operate Without Taking Commissions into Account

Trading without taking commissions into account is a mistake that many traders make, especially those who are just starting out in the world of trading. At first glance, commissions may seem like a minor cost, insignificant compared to the potential profits from a trade. However, this thinking can be misleading and lead to a significant impact on a trader's overall performance. Commissions, although small on each individual trade, add up over time, and if not managed properly, can erode profits and even turn winning trades into losing ones.

To understand the impact of commissions, it is important to consider the frequency with which a trader makes trades. Actively trading traders, such as day traders or scalpers, make many trades in a short period of time. Each of these transactions incurs a commission, which is charged for each purchase and sale made. Although these individual commissions may seem small, when added up at the end of a day, week or month, they can represent a considerable portion of a trader's capital. This is especially true if the trades are made in markets where commissions are relatively high or if the trading volume is high.

Another aspect to consider is that commissions not only affect profits, but also increase losses. When a trader opens a position, he is already at a disadvantage due to the commissions he must pay. This means that for a trade to be profitable, it must not only cover the cost of the commission, but also generate enough profit to offset that additional expense. If a trader ignores commissions and does not include them in his profitability calculation, he could end up trading under the false impression that he is making money, when in reality, after deducting commissions, he is losing.

Additionally, commissions can affect a trader's strategy. For example, a strategy that works well in theory or in a commission-free trading simulator may not be profitable in practice due to the associated costs. This is particularly relevant for traders using high-frequency strategies, where small differences in transaction costs can make the difference between success and failure. A strategy that produces small profits on each trade can be completely nullified by commissions if this factor has not been taken into account from the beginning.

It is also important to note that commissions vary depending on the type of asset and the broker used. Some brokers charge fixed commissions per trade, while others charge variable commissions based on the volume of the transaction or the type of asset traded. Additionally, some markets, such as stocks, tend to have higher commissions than others, such as forex or cryptocurrencies. This means that traders should be aware of the specific fees that apply to the markets they trade and adjust their strategy accordingly. Trading without taking these variations into account can lead to unexpected results and negatively affect long-term profitability.

Another common commission-related mistake is ignoring additional costs that may be associated with certain trades, such as spreads and maintenance or inactivity fees. The spread is the difference between the purchase price and the sale price of an asset, and represents an additional cost that the trader must overcome to obtain profits. Although it is not a direct commission, the spread has a similar effect on the profitability of a trade. Some brokers also charge additional fees if a trader keeps positions open overnight or does not trade for a certain period of time. These costs may seem minor, but if they add up, they can significantly reduce profits.

In addition to commissions and other costs, traders should consider how these expenses affect their long-term capital. As commissions accumulate, they reduce the capital available for trading, which in turn can limit a trader's ability to take advantage of new opportunities in the market. In the worst case, a trader who ignores the impact of commissions may find himself in a situation where, despite making successful trades, his capital gradually decreases due to the associated costs. This can be particularly detrimental to traders with small accounts, where every penny counts.

A smart approach to managing commissions is to include them in the planning and evaluation of each trade. Before opening a position, a trader must calculate not only the potential for profit and loss, but also the cost of commissions and other expenses. This allows you to make more informed decisions and avoid unpleasant surprises. Additionally, it is useful to periodically review the total costs associated with trading and evaluate whether the strategy used is still profitable after deducting all commissions. If it is found that commissions are having a significant negative impact, it may be necessary to adjust the strategy, switch to a broker with more competitive fees or even reconsider the trading style.

Finally, it is important to remember that commissions are an inevitable part of trading, but that does not mean they should be ignored. Traders who are successful in the long term are those who recognize and manage all the costs associated with their activity, including commissions. By including commissions in the analysis of each trade and overall planning, traders can ensure that their decisions are profitable and sustainable over time. In short, trading without considering commissions is like driving a car without considering the cost of fuel. It may seem like a minor detail at first, but over time, those costs add up and can make a big difference in the bottom line. By being aware of commissions and managing them properly, a trader can improve his chances of success and ensure that his efforts in the market are truly worthwhile.

Lack of Patience

Lack of patience is a silent but powerful enemy in the world of trading. It is a mistake that many traders make, often without even realizing it, and it can lead to impulsive and costly decisions. In an environment as dynamic as the financial market, where asset prices constantly fluctuate, impatience can cause a trader to enter or exit a trade at the wrong time, often resulting in losses that could have been avoided with a a little more calm and reflection.

One of the most important aspects of trading is knowing how to wait. Often the best opportunities don't present themselves immediately; They require time to develop. However, many traders, especially those who are new to the market, feel a constant urge to be active, to do something. This desire for action can lead them to make hasty decisions, such as entering a trade without waiting for all of their strategy criteria to be met, or closing a position too soon for fear of missing out on a profit that appears to be slipping away. This type of impatience is detrimental because it causes the trader to act reactively instead of proactively, thus losing control over their decision-making process.

Lack of patience also manifests itself in the unrealistic expectation of obtaining quick results. Many traders enter the market hoping to make quick money, inspired by the success stories of others or by advertising promising easy profits. However, the reality of trading is very different. Success in the financial markets is rarely instantaneous; It is the result of a gradual process of learning, adaptation and skill development. Traders who do not have the patience to go through this process often become discouraged quickly when they do not see immediate results, which can lead them to abandon their plans, constantly change strategies, or even stop trading altogether.

Another problem associated with a lack of patience is the tendency to overtrade. When a trader does not have the patience to wait for the correct setups, he may be tempted to enter trades that do not completely meet his criteria. This is known as "forcing" operations. Instead of patiently waiting for an opportunity that has a high potential for success, the trader jumps into any market movement in the hope of making a quick profit. This approach, however, often leads to losses, as trades made without a solid foundation tend to be riskier and less likely to be successful.

Additionally, a lack of patience can negatively impact a trader's ability to withstand inevitable market fluctuations. Financial markets are inherently volatile, and asset prices can rise and fall in a matter of minutes or hours. An impatient trader may panic when he sees that a position temporarily goes against his expectations, and close the trade prematurely to avoid a loss. However, in many cases, if he had been patient enough to wait, the market could have reversed the trend and the trade could have ended in profit. Patience is therefore an essential quality to withstand market volatility and allow trades to proceed as expected.

Lack of patience can also lead a trader to ignore his trading plan. A good trading plan includes specific rules about when to enter and exit a trade, as well as risk management. However, an impatient trader may be tempted to bypass these rules in an attempt to speed up results. For example, he may enter a trade before all the conditions of his strategy are met, or exit before reaching his profit target. This lack of discipline due to impatience not only increases the risk of losses, but also causes the trader to lose consistency in his approach, which is key to long-term success.

Additionally, impatience can cause a trader to focus too much on the short term, losing sight of the bigger picture. Instead of thinking in terms of weeks, months, or even years, an impatient trader may obsess over what is happening in the market right now, trying to capitalize on every small price movement. This short-term focus can be exhausting and often counterproductive, as markets often move in broader cycles that cannot be properly taken advantage of if you are too focused on daily fluctuations. A more patient and strategic approach allows the trader to take advantage of larger trends and achieve more significant returns over time.

Patience is also crucial when it comes to learning and improving at trading. Like any other skill, mastering trading requires time, practice and experience. Impatient traders often hope to dominate the market in a short period of time, which can lead to frustrations and disappointments when things don't go as planned. Instead of learning from their mistakes and continuing to improve, these traders may give up prematurely or jump from one strategy to another in search of a magic formula for success. The reality is that there are no shortcuts in trading; It takes time to develop a deep understanding of the market, to adjust and refine strategies, and to learn to manage the emotions that inevitably arise during the process.

Finally, a lack of patience can affect a trader's mindset. Trading is an emotionally demanding activity, and impatience can lead to a negative state of mind, characterized by anxiety, stress and frustration. These emotional states can cloud a trader's judgment and lead them to make irrational decisions. On the contrary, patience allows you to remain calm and mentally clear, which is crucial for making informed and rational decisions in the market. Patient traders are able to wait for the right moment to act, which often results in better decisions and greater long-term success.

In short, lack of patience is a common but devastating mistake in trading. It can lead to impulsive decisions, a loss of discipline, and an overly focused focus on the short term, all of which can erode profits and increase the risk of losses. Patience, on the other hand, allows traders to wait for the best opportunities, follow their plans consistently, and maintain a positive and focused mindset. Learning to be patient is not easy, especially in an environment as dynamic as the financial market, but it is an essential skill for any trader who aspires to long-term success.

Adrianne Morel

Not Accepting Errors

Not accepting mistakes is one of the biggest obstacles a trader can face on their path to success. In trading, as in life, making mistakes is inevitable. However, what really separates successful traders from unsuccessful ones is how they react to those mistakes. Many traders, especially those who are just starting out, fall into the trap of denying or minimizing their mistakes, rather than facing them head on. This denial may seem like a way to protect yourself from pain or frustration, but in reality, it only exacerbates problems and makes it difficult to learn and grow.

One of the main reasons why traders do not accept their mistakes is the fear of failure. Admitting a mistake can feel like admitting that you're not good enough, that you don't have what it takes to succeed in the marketplace. This fear can be so powerful that some traders choose to ignore their mistakes or look for external excuses, such as blaming the market, the news, or anything else outside of their control. However, this attitude is harmful, because by not accepting responsibility for their actions, traders deprive themselves of the opportunity to learn from their mistakes and improve their skills.

Another problem associated with not accepting mistakes is that it can lead to repeating the same mistakes over and over again. If a trader does not recognize that a decision was wrong, it is likely that he will continue making the same mistake in the future. For example, if a trader does not admit that he did not follow his trading plan on a losing trade, he could do the same again on the next trade, with the same negative results. This lack of self-criticism can lead to a vicious cycle of loss and frustration, which can be difficult to break without honest reflection and a willingness to change.

Accepting mistakes is also essential for developing a growth mindset. Trading is an activity in which continuous learning is essential. Every mistake, every loss, is an opportunity to learn something new, to adjust a strategy, or to improve in some aspect. However, this learning is only possible if the trader is willing to accept that he made a mistake in the first place. Those who deny or minimize their mistakes close themselves off from these learning opportunities and, as a result, their progress is hindered. Accepting mistakes, on the other hand, opens the door to learning and growth, which is crucial for long-term success.

Furthermore, not accepting mistakes can negatively affect a trader's confidence. When a trader denies or ignores his mistakes, deep down he knows that he is avoiding facing reality. This avoidance can create a feeling of insecurity, because the trader knows, although he does not want to admit it, that he is not dealing with the problems effectively. This insecurity can manifest itself in dubious trading decisions, a lack of conviction when following a trading plan, or a tendency to abandon trades early for fear of making another mistake. On the contrary, traders who accept and learn from their mistakes develop stronger, reality-based confidence, because they know they are improving and growing with each experience.

It is also important to note that accepting mistakes does not mean being harsh or critical of oneself in a destructive way. It's natural to feel bad after a losing trade or mistake, but what really matters is how you handle that situation. Instead of beating themselves up or falling into despair, a trader should see the mistake as an opportunity to learn and improve. Self-compassion and constructive self-criticism are essential in this process. You need to analyze what went wrong, identify the causes of the error, and think of ways to prevent it from happening again in the future. This proactive approach is much more beneficial than simply denying or ignoring the problem.

Furthermore, accepting mistakes helps a trader develop greater emotional resilience. Trading can be emotionally draining, especially when things don't go as planned. Traders who do not accept their mistakes often feel overwhelmed by guilt, frustration or regret, emotions that can be debilitating and can negatively affect their performance. However, those who accept and learn from their mistakes are better able to manage these emotions in a healthy way. They develop a greater ability to bounce back from losses, to remain calm under pressure, and to move forward with a positive, focused attitude.

Another crucial aspect of accepting mistakes is the importance of honesty with yourself. Trading requires a constant and honest evaluation of one's own skills, decisions and results. Traders who are honest with themselves about their mistakes are in a better position to make necessary adjustments and improve over time. This honesty also helps build a healthier relationship with the market, based on reality rather than unrealistic expectations or denials. When a trader is honest with himself, he can see the market more clearly, make more informed decisions and, ultimately, obtain better results.

Finally, accepting mistakes is a sign of maturity in trading. Experienced traders understand that mistakes are part of the process and there is no shame in making them. The important thing is how you respond to those errors. Traders who have reached a sufficient level of maturity are not scared by losses or mistakes, but rather see them as an inevitable part of the journey to success. This mature attitude allows them to stay focused on their long-term goals, without being derailed by temporary setbacks.

In conclusion, not accepting mistakes is one of the biggest barriers to success in trading. By refusing to face mistakes, traders deprive themselves of the opportunity to learn, grow, and improve. Accepting mistakes, on the other hand, allows for continuous learning, greater confidence, emotional resilience, and a growth mindset. It is an essential step for any trader who aspires to long-term success in the financial markets. By embracing mistakes as part of the process, traders can turn every setback into an opportunity to move forward and get closer to their goals.

The Power of Discipline

Discipline is, without a doubt, one of the fundamental pillars for success in trading. Without discipline, even the best strategies can fail, and even the most talented traders can see their efforts unravel. Discipline is what allows a trader to stay the course, follow their trading plan, and resist the temptation to make impulsive decisions that often lead to losses. In essence, discipline is the foundation upon which a successful and sustainable approach to financial markets is built.

When starting out in the world of trading, it is common to feel a mix of excitement and anxiety. The possibility of making money can be intoxicating, and this initial euphoria can cause many traders to jump into the market without a clear plan or without following the rules that have been proposed. This is where discipline plays a crucial role. A disciplined trader does not get carried away by the emotions of the moment. Instead, he follows his carefully crafted strategy, without deviating from it, even when the market seems to be offering irresistible opportunities for a quick profit.

A key aspect of trading discipline is the ability to follow a trading plan to the letter. A good trading plan is like a map that guides the trader through the complexities of the market, establishing when to enter and exit a trade, how much capital to risk, and how to manage risk. However, creating a plan is only the first step. The true test of a trader is his ability to stick to that plan even when things don't go as expected. It's easy to deviate from a plan when emotions are at play, but discipline requires resisting that temptation and trusting the process.

Discipline also manifests itself in a trader's ability to manage his emotions. Trading is an emotionally intense activity. Market fluctuations can cause feelings of euphoria when trades go well, or despair and fear when things take an unexpected turn. Without discipline, these feelings can lead a trader to make impulsive decisions, such as closing a trade prematurely for fear of a loss, or increasing the size of a position in a desperate attempt to recover lost money. Discipline, however, allows the trader to remain calm and mentally clear, making decisions based on his plan and analysis of it, rather than being carried away by panic or greed.

Another fundamental aspect of discipline is patience. Patience is essential in trading because opportunities do not always present themselves immediately. A disciplined trader knows how to wait. He does not rush into operations without all the conditions of his strategy having been met. This patient approach reduces the risk of loss and increases the chances of success, as the trader only enters trades that have a high return potential. Discipline and patience go hand in hand; Without one, the other cannot exist.

Discipline is also vital when it comes to risk management. Every operation in the market carries a certain level of risk, and one of the biggest mistakes a trader can make is underestimating that risk. A disciplined trader will never risk more than he is willing to lose in a single trade. This prudent approach ensures that a series of losing trades does not devastate the trading account. Discipline in risk management also involves the consistent use of stop-loss and take-profit, tools that help protect profits and limit losses. Without this discipline, a trader might be tempted to let losses run in the hope that the market will recover, which often results in even larger losses.

Additionally, discipline is crucial to avoid overtrading, a common trading mistake. Overtrading occurs when a trader makes too many trades in a short period of time, often due to impatience or the need to "do something." However, more trades do not necessarily mean more profits. In fact, overtrading often leads to losses because the trader is not waiting for the best opportunities, but rather is trading for the sake of trading. Discipline helps a trader to be selective, to choose only those trades that meet the criteria of his strategy and offer the best potential for success.

Consistency is another component of trading discipline. Consistency means following the same rules and principles on every trade, regardless of whether the market is going up or down. A disciplined trader does not change his approach mid-course, nor modify his trading plan based on the emotions of the moment. Consistency allows the performance of a strategy to be evaluated objectively, since decisions are made according to a clear set of rules. Without consistency, it's hard to know if a strategy is truly effective, because results will be skewed by impulsive decisions or changes in focus.

Self-discipline, or the ability to control one's impulses, is perhaps the most difficult, but most important, form of discipline in trading. Self-discipline requires strong willpower to keep going even when the going gets tough, to resist the temptation to abandon a plan when it doesn't seem to be working, and to stay focused on long-term goals rather than seeking instant gratification. . Self-discipline is what separates successful traders from those who fail, because it allows you to overcome inevitable challenges and continue to improve.

Discipline also involves the willingness to accept losses. In trading, not every trade will be a winner, and a disciplined trader knows this. Instead of trying to avoid losses at all costs, which often leads to irrational decisions, a disciplined trader accepts that losses are part of the process. The important thing is that these losses are controlled and limited, and that they do not endanger the total capital. The discipline in accepting losses and following through with the plan is what allows a trader to stay in the game for the long term.

Finally, discipline is a habit that develops over time. It is not something that can be acquired overnight. It requires practice, dedication, and a constant commitment to improvement. As a trader gains experience, he also develops the discipline necessary to trade successfully. This development is an ongoing process, and there is always room for improvement. Even the most experienced traders must constantly work on maintaining and strengthening their discipline, because in trading, a single moment of indiscipline can have significant consequences.

In short, the power of discipline in trading cannot be underestimated. It is the key to following a trading plan, managing risk, controlling emotions, and trading consistently and patiently. Without discipline, even the best strategy will fail. With discipline, a trader can navigate the complexities of the market with confidence, knowing that he is making informed and controlled decisions. By developing and maintaining discipline, a trader ensures that he is on the right path to success in the financial markets. Discipline is ultimately what transforms potential into results, and what turns an average trader into a successful one.